Contents

Cottage Tea Cosy

This charming tea cosy is easy to create with fusible web appliqué.

YOU WILL NEED

FABRIC FOR TEA COSY FRONT, BACK AND LINING:
One piece 14in x 10in (35.5cm x 25.5cm) for the roof
One piece 14in x 12in (35.5cm x 30.5cm) for the house
One piece 14in x 12in (35.5cm x 30.5cm) for the lining

Scraps of fabric for appliqué

OTHER MATERIALS
Fusible web
Wadding (batting)
Black and cream sewing thread
Ribbon and two buttons

Directions

1 Trace and transfer the tea cosy templates on to your chosen fabrics and cut out the front (roof and house), back (roof and house) and linings.

2 Using the templates, trace the roof, windows and door shapes on the paper side of the fusible web and cut out roughly. Iron the pieces onto the back of your chosen fabrics and cut out neatly. Remove the backing paper and position the motifs, glue side down, onto the cosy front. Iron in place. Machine stitch around the motifs using a medium-length stitch and contrasting thread.

3 Sew crosses on the windows to represent panes of glass. Sew lines across the roof for tiles, and down the door for panels.

4 Pin the cosy front and the cosy back to the wadding; cut out and machine stitch using a ³⁄₈in (1cm) seam allowance. Pin the front and back together, right sides facing. Insert and pin a loop of ribbon between the top seams, facing inwards. Machine stitch together, using a ³⁄₈in (1cm) seam allowance, leaving the bottom open. Trim the seams and turn through.

5 Pin the lining front and back together and machine stitch around the sides using a ³⁄₈in (1cm) seam allowance. Leaving the lining wrong side out, pull it over the cosy and then pin, matching side seams and lower raw edges.

6 Machine stitch around the lower edge of the cosy, leaving a 4in (10cm) gap at the back. Turn through to the right side and slip stitch the gap closed. Sew a button to the door for a handle and to the base of the ribbon loop.

Quilted Coasters

This coaster pattern is so easy to create and quilt that you'll find making a set of six or more no trouble at all.

YOU WILL NEED

FABRICS FOR COASTER TOP:

From white four 2¼in (5.7cm) squares

From a print two 2¼in (5.7cm) squares

From another print two 2¼in (5.7cm) squares

From polka dot one 2¼in (5.7cm) square

FABRIC FOR COASTER BACK:

One 6in (15.2cm) square

OTHER MATERIALS

Wadding (batting)

Dark pink and green stranded cotton (floss)

Directions

1 Take the four polka dot squares, the four print squares and the white square and arrange as shown in the photograph. Using ¼in (6mm) seams, sew the nine squares together. Press the seams.

2 Copy the quilting pattern and tape it to a window. Tape the patchwork on top, right side up, so the pattern shows through in the middle of the patchwork. Use a pencil to lightly trace the quilting pattern onto the fabric.

3 Take the 6in (15.2cm) square of wadding and safety pin on the back of the patchwork. Hand quilt using three strands of stranded cotton. Start with a dark pink French knot in the flower centre, then quilt the traced pattern, stitching through both layers, working the flowers in dark pink and leaves in green.

4 Place the patchwork right side up. Put the square of backing fabric right side down on top of the patchwork and pin together.

5 Trim the wadding and backing to the same size as the patchwork. Machine stitch together all the way around the edge leaving a gap of about 2in (5cm) in one side. Trim the corners a little, turn through to the right side and press.

6 Turn the edges of the gap inwards neatly and hand sew together with little stitches and matching thread. Machine sew all around the edge of the mat for a neat, firm edge.

Mini Squares Cushion

This smart cushion uses simple patchwork and modern fabrics for a lovely fresh look.

YOU WILL NEED

FAT QUARTER FABRIC PACK:

About five or six different prints for the cushion front, backing and back

OTHER MATERIALS

White sewing thread

Directions

1 For the patchwork on the cushion front, make a card template measuring 2in (5cm) square.

2 From the different prints cut a total of sixty-four squares of fabric, using the template (or use rotary cutting equipment instead if you have it). Pin the squares together along one edge, with right sides facing, to make a strip of eight patches. Machine stitch together, using a ⅜in (1cm) seam allowance. Repeat to make seven more strips of eight patches. Press open the seams.

3 Pin two strips together along one long edge, right sides facing and matching seam lines exactly. Machine stitch together. Repeat to join the rest of the strips together, to form a square of eight rows of eight patches. This is the cushion front.

4 Cut a piece of backing fabric the same size as the cushion front. Machine stitch the pieced front to the backing fabric, using a ⅜in (1cm) seam allowance.

5 For an envelope back, cut two pieces of fabric to the same height and two-thirds of the width of the cushion front. Press under a double ½in (1.3cm) hem down one long side of each; machine stitch in place.

6 Pin the backs to the cushion front with right sides facing overlapping the hemmed edges to fit. Machine stitch all the way around with a ½in (1.3cm) seam allowance. Trim corners and turn through.

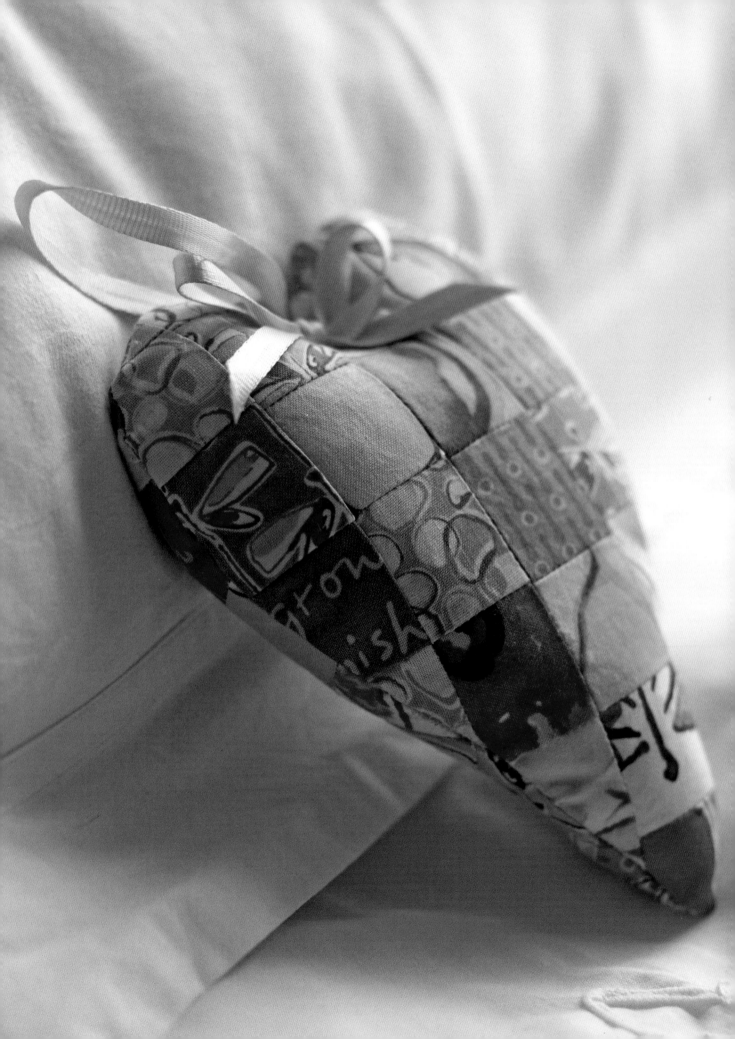

Lavender Heart

A heart-shaped sachet filled with sweet-smelling lavender makes a lovely gift.

YOU WILL NEED

CHARM SQUARE PACK OR A FABRIC DESIGN ROLL

OTHER MATERIALS
White sewing thread
Pink ribbon
Dried lavender and toy filling

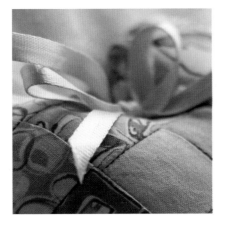

Directions

1 Make a card template measuring 1⅜in (3.5cm) square, and use to cut out seventy squares in various fabrics (or use rotary cutting equipment instead if you have it). Lay out the squares in your preferred order to form a rectangle ten squares wide x seven squares tall.

2 Take the first two squares in row 1 and with right sides facing stitch them together using a ¼in (6mm) seam. Add the third square and so on, until all seven squares are sewn together. Press the seams. Repeat this with all the rows.

3 Now sew the rows together, placing row 1 and row 2 right sides together and sewing with a ¼in (6mm) seam. Add the rest of the rows in the same way and press the seams.

4 You now have a rectangle of patchwork from which to cut your heart shape. With right sides facing, fold the fabric in half, short sides together and pin. Place the heart template on the patchwork piece and draw around it with a pencil. This is your stitching line.

5 Starting halfway along one side, machine stitch around the marked pencil line, taking great care with the curves, and leaving a 2in (5cm) gap for turning.

6 Cut out the heart shape ¼in (6mm) from the stitched line. Snip into the curves and down into the V to get the best possible shape, and turn right side out. Gently press into shape, stuff with toy stuffing and dried lavender. Sew the gap closed using slip stitch. Stitch a ribbon loop and bow at the top of the heart to hang.

Juggling Balls

A set of three colourful juggling balls makes a great present for a child, or anyone young at heart.

YOU WILL NEED

SELECTION OF 5IN (12.7CM) SQUARES:

at least four different fabrics

OTHER MATERIALS

Burgundy sewing thread
100g (4oz) dried pulses for stuffing

Directions

1 The fabric you use for making the juggling balls must be a tight cotton weave. Choose four different colours and press flat.

2 Use the juggling ball template to cut four panels from each of your chosen fabrics. You need four panels for each ball but choose a different fabric for each panel.

3 Now start to piece the panel pieces for each ball together. Lay two panels on top of each other, right sides facing, and pin together. Using a ½in (1.3cm) seam allowance, stitch along one edge following the shape of the curve; double stitch for extra security.

4 Repeat for the two remaining panels. Pin the two joined panels together, right sides facing. Stitch around the edges so that the four panels are stitched together, leaving a gap for turning and stuffing of about 1¼in (3.2cm). You now have an inside-out flat ball.

5 Turn the ball the right way and poke out the edges with a pencil. Using a funnel, stuff the ball tightly with dried pulses. Fold the edges of the turning gap neatly in and stitch closed using an invisible ladder stitch.

6 Repeat steps 3–5 to make two more balls, or more if you want.

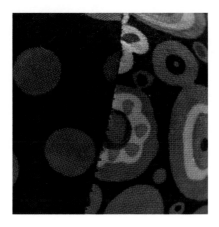

Quilted Oven Glove

This oven glove has a nice retro feel and is sure to come in handy in any kitchen.

YOU WILL NEED

FABRIC FOR GLOVE AND LINING:

Two coordinating prints

OTHER MATERIALS

White sewing thread
Insulating wadding (batting)
Ribbon

Directions

1 On a sheet of paper, draw loosely around the shape of your hand adding an extra 2in (5cm) all around and making sure it comes as far down your wrist as you'd like. Cut this out to make your oven glove template.

2 Fold the fabric in half, place the template on the folded fabric and draw around it to give you a front and a back glove. Cut out both shapes. Use your template to cut out a front and back piece from the insulating wadding and also a front and back from the lining fabric.

3 Tack (baste) the matching top and lining fabric pieces together with the wadding sandwiched in the middle. Quilt the fabric – crisscross lines are simple and effective.

4 With right sides facing, pin the quilted front and back pieces together, adding a loop of ribbon between the layers, making sure that the looped ends are facing inwards. Machine stitch together, taking extra care where the thumb meets the rest of the glove.

5 Snip into the seams around the thumb and turn the glove right way out.

6 Cut a 4in (10.2cm) wide strip of the lining fabric to bind the raw edge of the glove. Fold the fabric strip in half lengthways and press. Open up the strip and place one raw edge to the raw edge of the glove and stitch about ½in (1.3cm) from the edge. Fold the strip back over to the inside of the glove, turn under and stitch in place.

Patchwork Table Mat

Hand quilting creates a pretty table mat to enhance your home.

YOU WILL NEED

PATTERNED FABRIC FOR MAT TOP:

Ten 2¾in (7cm) squares

WHITE FABRIC FOR MAT TOP:

Two pieces 2¾in x 11¾in (7cm x 29.8cm)

FABRIC FOR MAT CENTRE AND BACKING:

One piece 8½in x 11¾in (16.5cm x 29.8cm)
One piece 12in x 18in (30.5cm x 45.7cm)

WADDING (BATTING):

One piece 12in x 18in (30.5cm x 45.7cm)

OTHER MATERIALS

White sewing thread
Blue, red-orange and green stranded cotton (floss)

Directions

1 To create the patchwork, take five of the 2¼in (7cm) print squares and using ¼in (6mm) seams, sew the squares together. Press seams in one direction. Do the same with the other five squares, changing the order if desired. Take the two strips of white fabric and sew one to the right side of one set of print squares and the other to the left side of the other set of print squares. Press the seams. Now take the pale print fabric piece, sew it to the white strips and press seams.

2 To hand quilt the mat, use the template provided. Copy the template and tape it to a bright window. Tape the patchwork on top, right side up, so the pattern shows through one of the white fabric strips. Use a pencil to lightly trace the pattern onto the fabric. Now copy the pattern onto the other white strip. Place the piece of wadding on the back of the patchwork and safety pin in place. Quilt through both layers using three strands of stranded cotton. Quilt the flower outlines in blue, the inner circle in red-orange and the linking curves in green. Stitch the central cross as long stitches in green.

3 To machine quilt the mat, press it first and then using thread to match the fabrics, quilt by machine down the long seams, 'in the ditch'. Press the work.

4 To finish the mat, place the patchwork right side up. Place the backing fabric right side down on top and pin together. Trim the wadding and backing to the same size as the patchwork. Sew the pieces together all the way around the edge leaving a gap of about 5in (12.7cm) in the bottom. Trim the points off the corners a little, turn through to the right side and press the seam.

5 Turn the edges of the gap inwards neatly and hand sew together with little stitches and matching thread. Finish by using your sewing machine to sew all around the edge of the mat about ⅛in (3mm) from the edge all round. This is called topstitching and creates a neat, firm edge.

Striped Tote

Create this fabulous tote bag using quick and easy machine strip piecing.

YOU WILL NEED

FAT QUARTER FABRIC PACK (THREE FABRICS)

FABRIC FOR BAG LINING:
Two pieces 12in x 18½in
(30.5cm x 47cm)

OTHER MATERIALS:
White sewing thread
Pink ribbon

Directions

1 Choose three different fabrics and from each fabric piece, cut out four strips each 12in x 3½in (30.5cm x 8.9cm). You should end up with twelve strips in total, six for the front and six for the back of the bag. Decide on your preferred layout of the strips.

2 Pin the first two strips together, right sides facing. Using a ¼in (6mm) seam allowance, machine stitch along the edge and continue in the same way adding each strip until the first six strips have been sewn to form the front of your bag. Press seams open on the reverse, then press the front. Repeat for the bag back.

3 Put the patchwork back and front together with right sides facing. Pin around the three sides, making sure all seams match up, and leaving the top open. Machine stitch with a ¼in (6mm) seam allowance. Turn inside out and press in a ½in (1.3cm) hem at the top (wrong sides facing).

4 Place the lining pieces together with right sides facing. Pin, then machine stitch together just as you did for the main bag following step 3.

5 Put the lining in the main bag, align the pressed hems at the top and then pin.

6 To make the handles cut twelve 3½ in (8.9cm) pieces (six per handle) and make a patchwork strip. (You could make your handles longer if you prefer.) Press in half, long sides together and open. Press a ⅜in (1cm) hem along each long side. Fold the strip over so the hems meet, pin and then sew. Pin the handles between the lining and the main bag so they are the same distance from the sides. Topstitch all around the top edge of the bag.

Hearts Cushion

This pretty cushion in delicious pinks and reds uses easy patchwork and machine stitched appliqué for a romantic look.

YOU WILL NEED

FABRICS FOR CUSHION FRONT:

Seven different prints

FABRIC FOR CUSHION BACK:

One piece 10in x 15½in (25.4cm x 39.4cm)

One piece 8in x 15½in 20.3cm x 39.4cm)

OTHER MATERIALS:

Red and pink sewing thread

1yd (1m) lightweight interlining

Cushion pad 15in (38cm) square

Directions

1 Make a template from card measuring 3½in (8.9cm) square. Iron interlining onto the back of your print fabrics, then use the template to cut out twenty-five squares. Arrange the squares in a five x five grid.

2 Using the template, cut a heart from card and use to cut out thirteen hearts from your fabrics. Place the hearts on alternate squares and machine sew in place with a straight or zigzag stitch in a red or contrasting thread colour.

3 Sew the squares together in rows of five squares using ¼in (6mm) seam allowances. Press the seams open. Now sew all the rows together in the same way to form a square. Press the seams open.

4 To make the envelope back for the cushion cover, first fold over and stitch a narrow double hem down one long edge of each cushion back piece.

5 With right sides facing and outer edges aligned, pin the hemmed rectangles to the cushion front with the hemmed edges overlapping in the centre. Machine stitch together around the sides with a ¼in (6mm) seam allowance, using light pink thread. Remove the pins, then trim the corners to reduce bulk. Turn the cushion cover the right way out through the envelope back. Press and insert the cushion pad.

Country Table Runner

A country-style table runner used as a centrepiece to adorn a table or sideboard, and is both attractive and functional.

YOU WILL NEED

FABRIC FOR RUNNER FRONT AND ENDS:

One piece 9½in x 37in (24cm x 94cm)

Two pieces 3in x 37in (7.6cm x 94cm)

One piece 10½in (26.7cm) square

FABRIC FOR RUNNER BACK:

One piece 15in x 52in (38cm x 132cm)

OTHER MATERIALS:

Pink cotton lace

Narrow satin ribbon

Four large white buttons

Directions

1 To make the front of the runner, sew the narrow strips to either side of the wide strip using ¼in (6mm) seams. Lay the lace over the top where the strips join and machine stitch in place.

2 To make the pointed ends, take the square of fabric and cut it in half diagonally. Sew one triangle to the top of the runner and the other triangle to the bottom. Press seams.

3 Place the runner right side down on the right side of the backing fabric and trim the backing fabric to the same shape. Sew together all round the edge, leaving a gap for turning through. Turn through to the right side, press seams and stitch the gap closed. Topstitch around the edge of the runner about ⅛in (3mm) from the edge. Add quilting if desired.

4 Cut two lengths of ribbon approximately 30in (76cm) long and tie into large bows. Pin and hand sew to each end of runner. Sew the buttons on to the corners of the central panel to finish.

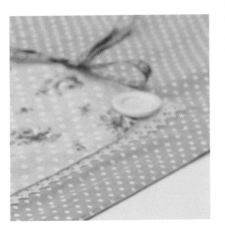

Flickering Star Pillow

Gorgeous fabrics and interesting patchwork give this flying geese design pillow a contemporary edge.

YOU WILL NEED

FABRIC FOR CUSHION FRONT:

Long quarter yd/m (solid white fabric)
One 5½in (14cm) square (fabric A)
Fat quarter (fabric B)
Fat quarter (fabric C)
Fat quarter (fabric D)
Fat quarter (fabric E)

FABRIC FOR CUSHION LINING:

One 24in (61cm) square

FABRIC FOR CUSHION BACK:

One 24in (61cm) square

OTHER MATERIALS:

White sewing thread
Wadding (batting) 24in (61cm) square

CUT YOUR FABRICS AS FOLLOWS:

From solid white fabric:

Two 6in (15.2cm) squares
Four 3½in (8.9cm) squares
Eight 3in (7.6cm) squares
Eight rectangles each 3in x 5½in (7.6cm x 14cm)

From fabric A:

One square 5½in (14cm)

From fabric B:

Two squares 6in (15.2cm)

From fabric C:

Four squares 3in (7.6cm)
Four rectangles each 3in x 5½in (7.6cm x 14cm)

From fabric D:

Four squares 3½in (8.9cm)
Eight squares 3in (7.6cm)

From fabric E:

Eight squares 3in (7.6cm)

Directions

1 Make four flying geese units using eight fabric E 3in (7.6cm) squares and four of the white 3in x 5½in (7.6cm x 14cm) rectangles. To make one unit, place a rectangle right side up, with a square right side down on top, aligning the shapes at the edges of the rectangle (see Fig 1). Pencil a line across the diagonal, then pin the shapes together and sew along the diagonal line. Press the square towards the corner so it becomes a triangle. Trim off excess fabric at the back. Add the other square to make a triangle on the other side of the rectangle. Make another three flying geese units.

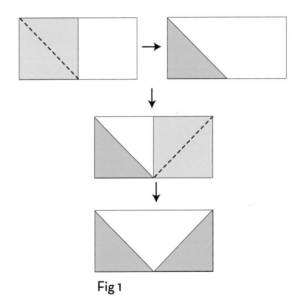

Fig 1

2 Trim the units to 3in x 5½in (7.6cm x 14cm). Using ¼in (6mm) seams, sew two units to the top and bottom of the fabric A 5½in (14cm) square. Sew a fabric C 3in (7.6cm) square to opposite sides of the remaining fabric E flying geese. Sew to the sides of the fabric A square.

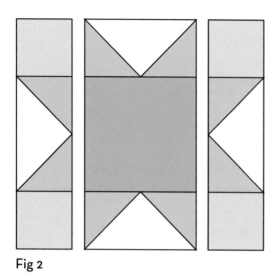

Fig 2

3 Make four flying geese units using eight fabric D 3in (7.6cm) squares and four of the white 3in x 5½in (7.6cm x 14cm) rectangles. Trim to 3in x 5½in (7.6cm x 14cm). Sew a white 3in 7.6cm) square to opposite sides of each of the flying geese.

4 Make eight half-square triangles using four fabric D 3½in (8.9cm) squares and four white 3½in (8.9cm) squares. To make one unit, place a fabric D square right sides together with a white square and mark the diagonal line (Fig 3A). Pin the squares together and sew ¼in (6mm) either side of the marked line (Fig 3B). These lines can be marked too if desired. Now cut the two triangles apart on the marked diagonal line (Fig 3C). Press the units to set the seams and then press open, usually towards the darker fabric (Fig 3D). Trim the unit to 3in (7.6cm) square. Make eight units in total.

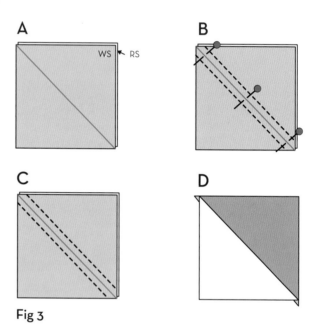

Fig 3

5 Sew half-square triangle units to opposite sides of the fabric C 3in x 5½in (7.6cm x 14cm) rectangles. Sew each of these units to the bottom of each of the fabric D flying geese units.

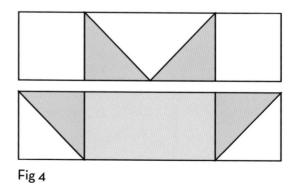

Fig 4

6 Sew two of the fabric D/C units to the top and bottom of the fabric A square.

7 Make four half-square triangles using two fabric B 6in (15.2cm) squares and two white 6in (15.2cm) squares. Trim to 5½in (14cm) square. Sew to opposite sides of two of the fabric D/C units. Sew to the sides of the fabric A square.

8 Layer the pillow top, wadding (batting) and lining fabric together and tack (baste) to keep the layers secure. Quilt as desired – quilting ¼in (6mm) from the seam lines is easy and looks very effective.

9 Finish the pillow using a backing of your choice. Place the backing fabric right sides together with the cushion front and sew together all round using a ¼in (6mm) seam, leaving a gap for turning through. Turn through to the right side and press seams. Insert a pillow pad. Turn the edges of the gap in neatly and slip stitch the edges together. Bind the edges of the pillow for a neat finish.

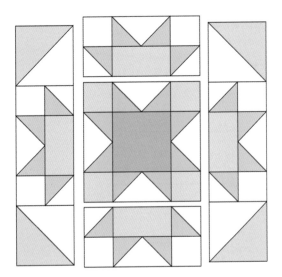

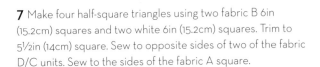

Fig 5

Templates

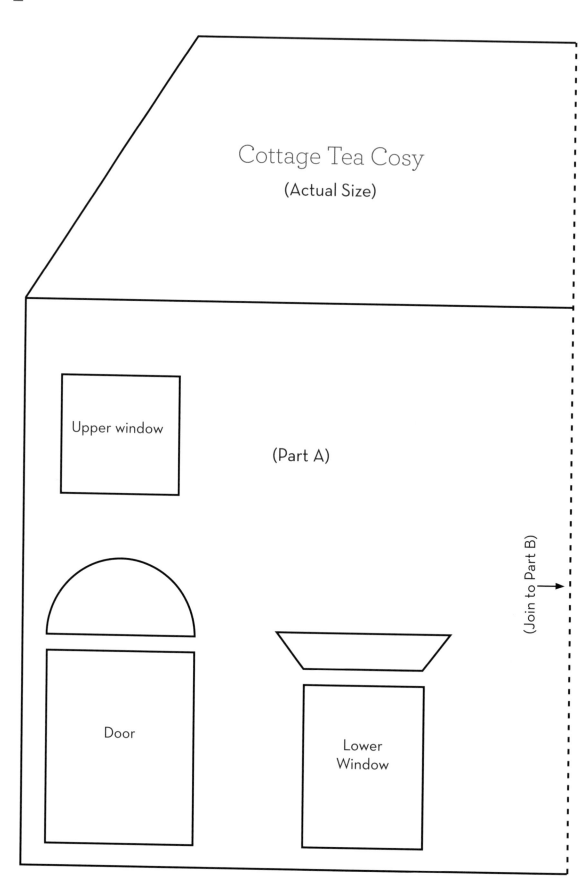

Cottage Tea Cosy

(Actual Size)

Upper window

(Part A)

(Join to Part B)

Door

Lower
Window

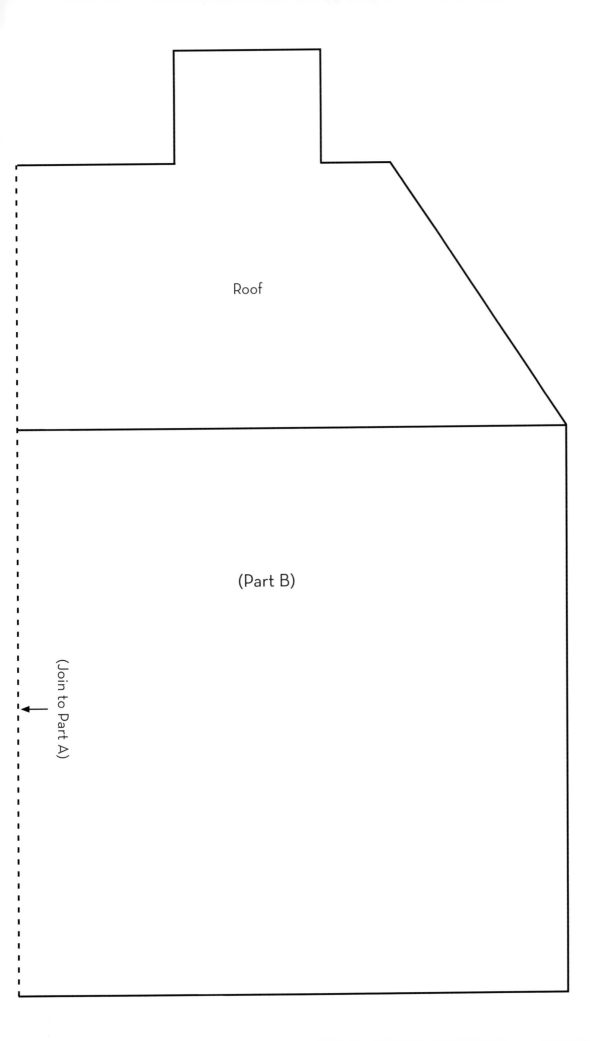

Roof

(Part B)

(Join to Part A)

Quilted Coasters

(Actual Size)

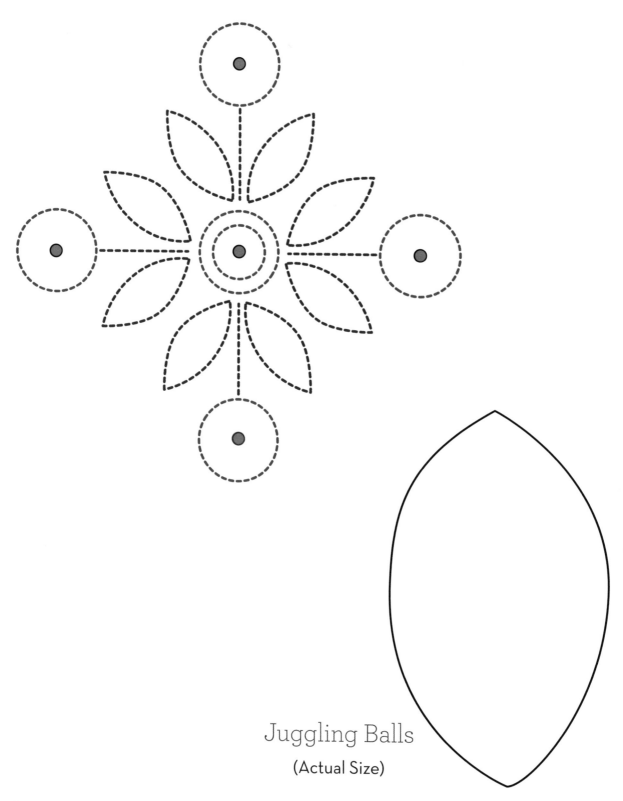

Juggling Balls

(Actual Size)

Lavender Heart

(Actual Size)

Gap for turning

Patchwork Table Mat

(Actual Size)

Hearts Cushion

(Actual Size)

Gallery

Bring a fresh, contemporary look to your home with this collection of easy-to-make projects. They would all make wonderful gifts too.

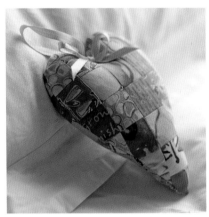

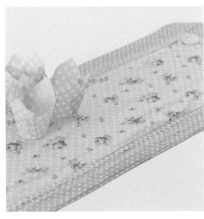

Contributors

Jenny Arnott	Linda Clements
Upinder Birdi	Marion Elliot
Tacha Breucher	Mary Fogg
Sarah Callard	Lisa Fordham

A DAVID & CHARLES BOOK
© F&W Media International, Ltd 2013

David & Charles is an imprint of F&W Media International, Ltd
Brunel House, Forde Close, Newton Abbot, TQ12 4PU, UK

F&W Media International, Ltd is a subsidiary of F+W Media, Inc
10151 Carver Road, Suite #200, Blue Ash, OH 45242, USA

Text and Designs © F&W Media International, Ltd 2013
Layout and Photography © F&W Media International, Ltd 2013

First published in the UK and USA in 2013

The author and publisher have made every effort to ensure that all the instructions in the book are accurate and safe, and therefore cannot accept liability for any resulting injury, damage or loss to persons or property, however it may arise.

Names of manufacturers and product ranges are provided for the information of readers, with no intention to infringe copyright or trademarks.

A catalogue record for this book is available from the British Library.

ISBN-13: 978-1-4463-0348-1 paperback
ISBN-10: 1-4463-0348-9 paperback

Printed in China by RR Donnelley for
F&W Media International, Ltd
Brunel House, Forde Close, Newton Abbot, TQ12 4PU, UK

10 9 8 7 6 5 4 3 2 1

F+W Media publishes high quality books on a wide range of subjects. For more great book ideas visit:
www.stitchcraftcreate.co.uk